# Let's Talk About

# CHEATING

# Let's Talk About
# CHEATING

## By JOY BERRY

*Illustrated by John Costanza*
*Edited by Orly Kelly*
*Designed by Jill Losson*

GROLIER ENTERPRISES CORP.

Let's talk about CHEATING.

Everyone who plays a competitive game wants to win. But everyone cannot win. If someone is going to win, someone else must lose.

No one likes to lose. Losing is not fun.

When you lose, you may think that it is because you are not so smart or so "good" as the person who won. You might think that you are dumb or "no good."

When you do not feel good about yourself,
you may think that you cannot do anything.
You might begin to feel that you will never win.

If you lose often, you may begin to think that you must CHEAT in order to win.

Breaking the rules dishonestly when you play a game is CHEATING.

*Before you decide to cheat, think about it.*

There are other things you can do to make sure that you win at least some of the time.

To begin with, you should try to play with someone who is somewhat *equal to you.*

This means that you should not always play with someone who is older or more experienced than you.

If you must play with someone who is older or more experienced than you, try to play games where skill and practice are not important. Play games that anyone can win. Then let luck decide who the winner will be.

Instead of cheating to win, try to play games that you know you have a chance to win.

Do not always play games that you know you are going to lose.

*Before you begin playing a game*, find out exactly what the rules are.

Make sure that the rules are understood by you and everyone who is playing with you.

Once you know what the rules are, follow them exactly.

Do not do anything that is against the rules.

Do not try to change the rules in the middle of a game.

*When you play a game* with someone, try to remember that you are playing for fun.

Winning should not be more important than having a good time. Try to enjoy the fun you are having while you are playing.

Don't worry about winning or losing.

If people cheat while you are playing a game with them, talk to them kindly about it.

Tell them that you know they are cheating. Ask them to stop it.

If people keep cheating after you have talked with them about it, do not play with them anymore.

No one likes to play with someone who cheats.

This is why you should not cheat. If you want people to play with you, you must not cheat.

Remember, no one wins all the time. When you do lose —

- do not think of yourself as a loser;
- do not think that you will never win;
- do not give up or stop trying;
- think about the things you are good at;
- remember the times you have won.

It is important to treat other people the way you want to be treated.

If you do not want other people to cheat, you must not cheat.